The Singing Pope

The Singing Pope

The Story of Pope John Paul II

Rinna Wolfe

The Seabury Press · New York

In memory
of my mother, Pauline,
Barbara and Ruth,
and to Viviana.

The Seabury Press
815 Second Avenue
New York, New York 10017

Library of Congress Cataloging in Publication Data
Wolfe, Rinna.   The Singing Pope.
SUMMARY: A biography of the former Polish cardinal
who was the first non-Italian to be elected Pope
since 1523.
1. John Paul II, Pope, 1920–   —Juvenile
literature. 2. Popes—Biography—Juvenile literature. [1. John Paul II, Pope, 1920–   2. Popes] I. Title
BX1378.5.W64   282'.092'4 [B] [92]   80-17531
ISBN 0-8164-0472-0

PHOTO CREDITS: Prologue, Chris Niedenthal/NC News; Chapter 1,
Chris Niedenthal/NC News; Chapter 2, M. Malinski; Chapter 3, M.
Malinski; Chapter 4, M. Malinski; Chapter 5, NC News/Interpress
Photos; Chapter 6, NC News; Chapter 7, Uzan/Gamma; Chapter 8, NC
News; Chapter 9, UPI; Chapter 10, Wide World/RNS; Chapter 11, NC
News; Chapter 12, Chris Sheridan; Chapter 13, Bob Kelly/NC News;
Chapter 14, Wide World; Chapter 15, Jack Spratt/NC News; Chapter 16,
Dennis Trowbridge/NC News; Chapter 17, Wide World. Photo Research:
Patricia Myers.

Contents

A Pronouncing Guide   vii

Prologue   1

1 · The Early Years   5

2 · The Student   13

3 · The Occupation   19

4 · Training and the Priesthood   27

5 · The Teacher and the Cardinal   37

6 · Nowa Huta-Vatican II   45

7 · Pope Paul VI   51

8 · The Conclave   57

9 · Pope John Paul I   63

10 · The New Pope   71

11 · Return to Poland   81

12 · Old World to New   87

13 · America's Heartland   97

14 · Washington, D.C.   101

15 · A Tragedy   105

16 · A Changing Church   109

17 · *Sto-Lat!*   117

A Pronouncing Guide

Many Polish names and words look unusual at first, but most of the sounds are quite similar to those of English. The difference lies in what letters are used to write the sounds. The Polish name or word will be given in the left hand column and the pronouncing guide for that name or word, in the right hand column. The following symbols are used in the pronouncing guide to describe the vowel sounds in the Polish words:

ă as in p<u>a</u>t	ĕ as in p<u>e</u>t	ī as in p<u>ie</u>
ā as in p<u>ay</u>	ē as in b<u>ee</u>	ō as in t<u>oe</u>
ä as in f<u>a</u>ther	ĭ as in p<u>i</u>t	o͞o as in f<u>oo</u>d

Częstochowa	chĕnstōhōvä
Debniki	dĕbnēkē
Jageillonian	yägēĕlōnēĕn
Kaczorowska	kächōrovskä
Koscielna	kōshchĕlnä
Kotlarczyk, Mieczyslaw	kōtlärchĭk, mēĕchĭswäv
Krakow	kräko͞ov
Kydrynski	kĭdrĭnskē
palant	pälänt
Sapieha	säpēĕhä
Tygodnik Powszechny	tĭgōdnēk pōvshĕhnĭ
Wadowice	vädōvētsĕ
Wawel	vävĕl
Wojtyla	vōētĭwä
Zedgadlowicz	zĕdgädwōvēch

Prologue

It looked like a parade, a circus and a huge Polish wedding all in one. Flowers covered lampposts, church spires, balconies, postmen's bicycles. Yellow and white banners (the papal colors) fluttered in the blue June sky. Church bells pealed continuously.

A plane circled over the Warsaw airport. Minutes later it landed. A burly figure dressed in a white robe stepped outside and knelt. He kissed the Polish earth.

Whisked into an open car, the man rode through cities and tiny towns. Everywhere teenagers rushed to touch him as though he were a rock star. Grandmothers in bright bandanas held babies up high to be kissed or blessed.

Standing shoulder to shoulder thousands of people surrounded him. They heard him make short speeches, tell bad jokes, and saw him hug old friends. They roared out traditional hymns and the world's

The people of Poland welcome John Paul II: a new pope, a new world hero, and a man they have known and loved for many years.

1

first Polish pope—and the youngest pope in 132 years—sang, too, in a deep baritone voice.

Everyone felt joy—joy in being Polish, joy in being human, and joy in being with Pope John Paul II who had returned to his homeland.

But Pope John Paul II had not always known so much joy. He had been poor. He had lived without freedom. So, on the day he returned to his homeland he returned, in part, to help people live better, more peaceful lives.

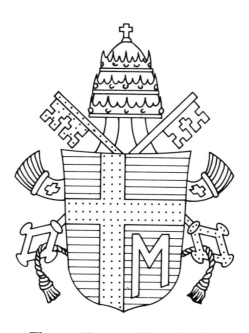

The papal arms of John Paul II
has the traditional three-tiered tiara
and crossed keys of all papal arms.
The tiara or crown represents
the pope's role as teacher, priest, and ruler.
The keys indicate his role
as successor to Saint Peter,
who was given the "Keys of the Kingdom."
Each pope chooses his own shield design,
and John Paul II decided to have
the same shield he had used as
Cardinal-Archbishop of Krakow.
The *M* in the lower right quadrant
represents the historic role
of the Virgin Mary in the life of the Church,
the pope's personal devotion to her,
and the role she has played
as Our Lady of Częstochowa in the lives
of the Polish people.

🎕1🎕

The Early Years

Karol Wojtyla was born on May 18, 1920, in quiet Wadowice. About thirty miles from the big city of Krakow, this town was so small neighbors knew each other well.

Once Wadowice had been ruled by dukes of Silesia and by a Polish king as well. For over 600 years when church bells chimed on Sundays, scrubbed-clean villagers trudged through the cobble-stone streets to the tall church that dominates the square. For many centuries Wadowice was and still is, a market town where farmers from nearby brought their wheat, potato, and beetroot crops to sell.

Life in Poland has always been difficult. The country is wedged between two forceful nations—Russia and Germany. For 123 years, foreigners ruled the Poles. In 1920, the year in which Karol was born, Poland had been an independent nation for just one and a half

This is the house in Wadowice, Poland, where Karol Wojtyla was born. The window (center) was in Karol's own room.

years. After many wars the Polish people were tired of fighting, and very poor.

Hardworking farmers grew crops on land they were not allowed to own. Shopkeepers and factory workers did humble jobs for low wages. Life was harsh. Everyone including the Wojtyla family struggled to survive.

The Wojtyla family lived in the corner stone building marked 7 Koscielna Street. A small gate swung into a dusty court. Running errands for their mother, *Lokek* (an affectionate name for Karol) and his brother Edmund (who was 15 years older than he), climbed the steep, crooked stone steps countless times to their first floor apartment.

The front door opened into a kitchen and two other rooms. The bathroom, like bathrooms of the other apartments, was separated by a main hall. One window overlooked the street. Three more windows faced the church which was next door. Karol learned to tell time by looking at the ancient sundial on the church wall.

Young Karol's father—for whom he was named— was a kind, religious man. During World War I he fought in the *Legions*. This volunteer group later became part of Poland's independent army. Promoted to captain, Karol's father worked for a while as a supply officer in the Wadowice garrison. When ill health forced him to retire, the family had to live on his small military pension.

Karol's Lithuanian mother Emilia (born Kaczorowska) was a school teacher before she married.

Her family spoke German so consequently this was the first language Karol heard. Although Emilia was not a strong woman, she shopped, cooked, washed, ironed, and took in sewing to make her husband's income stretch further. She kept the family apartment clean and cheerful.

Proud of her son, one neighbor remembers hearing Mrs. Wojtyla say, "You'll see. My Lokek will be a great man someday."

Gentle and playful, Karol Wojtyla made friends easily. A quick student, he loved school. He wrote and recited well and excelled in religious education, Latin, Greek, and German. Reading gave him special pleasure. Whenever he could he buried his nose in a book. Often he tutored classmates in school or in their homes.

A deeply religious family, the Wojtylas prayed together every day. When Karol became an altar boy he attended mass at seven in the morning and then hurried to class by eight o'clock. School lasted till four in the afternoon. Then Karol did his homework or helped his mother.

At times he liked to pretend he was celebrating mass. Placing two candles and a holy picture on the kitchen table, he would enlist two friends to act as altar boys. Then, dressed in a worsted cape that his mother made for him, he would bless his imaginary congregation.

Like most children, Karol loved to play outdoors. During the long summer twilight Karol's mother sat and chatted with village women near the well on the hill. Not too far away Karol, his friend Boguslaw Banas (the café owner's son) and other boys, practiced soccer in the street. Usually Karol played goalie and he was very good.

Sometimes Edmund took him to local soccer games. Seated atop his brother's shoulders Karol watched the action from a perfect position.

Sometimes the boys played *palant*. The object of this Polish game was to bounce a stick into the air and try to hit it with another one. On hot days the boys swam in the Skawa river. But Karol's favorite season was winter.

Karol loved the sharp wind against his face. He enjoyed throwing snowballs and rolling in the snow. But best of all he loved the sound of snow crunching beneath his feet when he skied down the low hills around the town.

Tragedy struck the Wojtylas unexpectedly when Karol was nine. His mother died of a heart ailment. When a neighbor tried to console Karol, she heard him say, "It was God's will." But he missed his mother for a long time.

Four years later, Edmund (who'd become a doctor) died during a scarlet fever epidemic.

Alone now the saddened pair, father and son, became inseparable good friends. Mr. Wojtyla raised his son single-handedly. He cooked, scrubbed, and mended his son's clothes.

Mr. Wojtyla was strict but he was also a warmhearted man. He had high standards and expected much of young Karol. A lover of education, he tutored Karol and checked his homework.

Mr. Wojtyla respected all people. Perhaps because of his army training he also demanded hard work and obedience. Karol needed just one look and he obeyed his father's wishes. Once Mr. Wojtyla left him alone in an unheated room to help him develop endurance. Karol understood his father's ways.

After school Karol often stopped in the basement café to see his friend Banas and his mother. After the boys played a while Karol went home to study and to eat the meal his father had prepared. Sometimes a neighbor invited the pair to eat with them. After dinner Karol and his father strolled along town streets talking together about everything. Bedtime came early because Karol never missed mass at seven in the morning.

At Christmas and Easter they visited Karol's aunt Stefania (his father's sister) who taught school.

Mieczyslaw Kotlarczyks was Karol's next door neighbor and a good friend, too. A designer of stage sets, he also taught literature in a local high school. He and his wife enjoyed Karol's chatty drop-in evening visits. They introduced him to the theatre. Ever ready and patient they always answered his questions. Karol watched and sometimes helped Mr. Kotlarczyks build stage sets.

Once, without thinking, Karol dashed into the apartment. He did not notice a set design that was lying on the floor until it was too late. His muddied boots had dirtied it. Before anyone could say a word, terribly upset, Karol removed his boots and cleaned up the mess.

The Kotlarczyks loved Karol. When the two families moved to Krakow, for a time they lived together, the Wojtylas and their friends. Certainly the couple inspired Karol with a life-long interest in acting. Later they joined together to found a theatrical group that kept Polish pride alive.

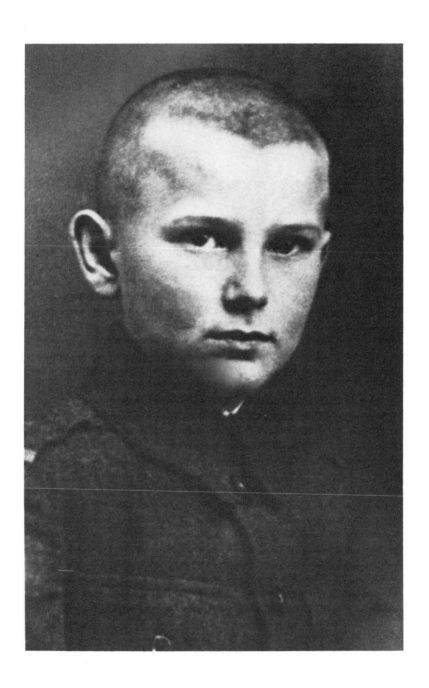

~❦ 2 ❦~

The Student

When Karol was 15 and his friend Boguslaw (Bogu) was 13, an almost fatal accident occurred. Bogu's father kept a revolver in his café cash drawer. It belonged to a policeman who knew that when he drank too much he could use it harmfully. So he had left the gun with Mr. Banas for safekeeping.

One day the two boys were playing alone in the café. Boguslaw took the revolver from the drawer. Jokingly he pointed it directly at Karol. Standing less than six feet away, he fired at Karol's heart. Somehow the bullet missed by a hair's sliver. Instead it broke the window behind him.

Awakened by the shot, Mr. Banas rushed into the room. Without a word to the scared, motionless boys, he put the revolver away. Karol did not mention the incident again either. But thirty-four years later, Boguslaw told a writer, "I still get goose flesh thinking, 'My God. I might have killed the pope'."

Like most Polish boys of his generation, Karol Wojtyla wore a school uniform and had his hair cut very short.

Karol loved people. Friends remember him as being handsome, athletic, kind, and full of good cheer. Some say he once had a steady girl friend. But for the most part he left girls alone.

Karol attended the local high school, a two floor building with large windows and small rooms. Originally named *Wadowica* for a rector of the 16th century, the town council later renamed it after the Polish poet-novelist *Zedgadlowicz.*

Karol was one of the first students to join a high school drama club where he both acted and directed. One time when they needed a substitute for someone who'd taken ill, by making a quick costume change, Karol managed to play two parts in the same show.

Karol played guitar. And often he and other teenagers gathered in the local park on Saturday nights to sing folk songs. He began writing poetry, and in his last year in high school won second prize reciting at a speech festival. People thought he was an exceptional fellow but he didn't put on airs about it.

Father Edward Zacher was Karol's religious teacher in high school. When asked how Karol behaved he said, "I cannot recall any penalty I had to give him. It is quite possible he did wrong things like any other boy, but it was nothing serious."

Father Zacher added, "His marks were not only good they were a mark higher. Karol did best in languages and letters." Yet as well liked as Karol was, as seemingly perfect a pupil he was, his teacher felt Karol was different. He was more thoughtful, more serious than the other students.

One day Adam, Cardinal Sapieha, a prince by birth and the archbishop of Krakow, visited the Wadowice parish. Karol, as the best student in the school, was asked to give the welcoming speech. Cardinal Sapieha was impressed.

In thanking Karol he said, "You seem to be a clever young man. Do you think you are going to be a priest?"

"No," Karol said. I am going to the university to study literature. And I'm also interested in theatre."

Father Zacher added, "Mr. Kotlarczyk is his hero."

"That's a pity. We need someone like him," the cardinal said. But Karol and the cardinal were destined to meet again.

In 1938 Karol graduated with honors. Soon after he and his father left for Krakow, the beautiful, ancient city called "the jewel of Poland."

They moved to Debniki, a quaint section of the city. Their basement apartment was dark and cramped. But neither of them complained. Karol found work with a road building crew. All through the summer he lifted and carted construction materials. In the fall he entered the Jagellonian University.

What a sense of history he must have felt! Finally he was a student at the same college where the astronomer Nicolas Copernicus had studied in the 15th century. He heard lectures in buildings that were more than 500 years old. He wrote papers till the wee morning hours. Occasionally he joined friends in discussion, drinking coffee with them in Krakow's cafés.

He became a member of the Polish Language Society and took elocution lessons. At one poetry reading he met Juliusz Kydrynski. Liking the same things, they saw plays together, shared their poetry, and eventually held prayer meetings and discussions in Kydrynski's flat. They became friends and have remained so.

Karol joined a group of students and young workers who produced amateur plays. During a Krakow summer festival in 1939 they presented *The Knight of the Moon*. The plot was simple. It told how a nobleman sold his soul and was sent by the devil to hell. But when he prayed he was freed and landed on the moon.

Karol played the role of his birthsign Taurus. He wore a costume that consisted of shorts, boxing gloves, and a Taurus mask (a bull's head). He spoke few lines but he said them with all the passion he felt for Polish theatre.

In this last untroubled year Karol wandered through Krakow's monasteries and churches. He studied the city monuments. Especially he lingered at the complex fortress Wawel Castle, that overlooked the Vistula River. He spent hours praying before its main altar. He stopped at the tombs of kings and religious and literary heroes buried there.

Karol enjoyed visiting the market square of the Old Town, near the castle. Like a tourist he looked at the church of St. Mary and listened to the Trumpeter of Krakow sound the hour. The call has always been left incomplete in memory of the famous Polish hero, the original trumpeter, who was killed by an enemy's arrow while sounding the alarm to besieged Krakow.

On the first Friday of each month, Karol helped serve mass in the Wawel cathedral. Karol's days and nights were very full.

❦ 3 ❦

The Occupation

Outside of Poland the rest of Europe rumbled with rumors of war. The German dictator Adolf Hitler readied to attack. At first Germany had the Soviet Union, one of Poland's traditional enemies, as its ally. The two dictatorships planned to take over the world. Karol and fellow students spent part of the summer taking basic training in a military camp.

Without warning, on September 1, 1939, Hitler broke a five year treaty. He ordered a *blitzkrieg* (speedy invasion) of Poland. Nazi tanks crossed the Polish border swiftly. Taken by surprise, only a third of the Polish army was prepared to fight. The Germans bombed the main cities and towns continuously. Within fifteen days Germany had conquered this small farming country.

Life under the German occupation was unbearable. The people of Krakow lived in terror. During the next two years millions of Poles—officers and soldiers, Jews,

Karol Wojtyla undoubtedly saw the grim wall go up around the Krakow ghetto in the darkest days of the German occupation.

priests, business people, professors, all disappeared. Some were sent to slave-labor camps. Others went to Auschwitz (the infamous concentration camp). The Nazis were ruthless.

People never knew when the Gestapo or police would round up innocent victims. People were imprisoned for being out after curfew, if they didn't have a work-permit, or for no reason at all. Father Waloszek, Karol's parish priest in Wadowice, died at Auschwitz.

The new regime ended all cultural activities. Religious training was forbidden. The Jageillonian University was closed.

One June day in 1940, the German leaders in Poland called the professors and teachers together. Supposedly they wanted to discuss reopening the college. But only those wise people who did not come, escaped. Krakow's professors were arrested and sent to concentration camps. Most of them never returned. The Germans were determined to make the Poles their slaves.

But threats could not stop Poles from learning. The students were just as determined. They decided to organize—not to kill Germans, but to continue their education. They established an underground university. Meeting secretly, they tutored one another, held classes in private apartments, and took exams which their professors graded. Karol enrolled for his second university year knowing full well the danger to his life if he were caught.

About 136 teachers risked their lives to teach more

than 800 students. Juliusz Kydrynski recalls that "once chairs were arranged for about 30 people. Then the Gestapo arrived. They were asking for somebody and they saw all the chairs. My mother said we were preparing for a party. This seemed to satisfy them, so they left. But that was a very close thing because often there were people sitting around waiting for a meeting to start. If the Gestapo had arrived when people were there, they would have thought we were plotting against them. . . . They were dangerous times for all of us."

At this time Karol began an unusual project with his old friend Kotlarczyk. Together they started the underground acting troupe called Rhapsody Theatre (or Theatre of the Spoken Word). Five actors, including Karol, rehearsed by candlelight in cold kitchens whenever they felt safe. According to Kydrynski, actors "moved from house to house, arriving or leaving singly or in pairs." Careful not to include possible informers, they only invited people they knew well. Karol and everybody else understood the risk they took.

The troupe performed without scenery. They were strong believers in freedom and Polish culture—and the power of the theater. They held over 100 rehearsals and gave 22 performances for friends in stores and private homes. Their performances kept Polish pride alive.

Karol had a tiring routine. Each morning he stopped at the local church to pray. Evenings he met with professors to study; or he rehearsed a Polish play. But he needed money to support his father. The Polish army pension had stopped with the German occupation. Besides he needed a job so he would not be deported to a labor camp in Germany. So Kydrynski found him work splitting stone in the Solvay quarry.

The winter was bitter. Temperatures dropping to 30 degrees below zero were usual. Karol and the other men smeared their faces with vaseline to prevent frostbite. Karol broke rocks with a sledgehammer and piled them into a wheelbarrow. Then he pushed the wheelbarrow to a railroad car and returned to break more rocks. Karol learned quickly to hit the stone so that chips would not fly into his face or eyes. But the work was hard.

Kydrynski wrote in a book, "In the winter I and Karol managed every now and then to step into a small hut heated with an iron stove. We were allowed to spend a quarter of an hour there, during our breakfast break. We brought from home slices of low quality rye bread, beetroot jam, and ersatz corn coffee in flasks."

The job was only bearable because older quarrymen befriended them and made their jobs easier when they could. The quarry foreman liked Karol so he "promoted" him to the more dangerous but less exhausting job of stringing fuses and packing explosives into rocks.

Karol worked days and studied nights. After work, in the late afternoon, he hunted for food and

22

coal to store in his cellar. One evening, on the way home, he collapsed from exhaustion. A passing German truck hit him and did not stop. Karol laid in the street all night with a fractured skull. In the morning the woman who found him brought Karol to the hospital. He spent several weeks recovering in a friend's house.

When he returned to work he had a new job, purifying the water used in the boilers. He carried so many buckets of lime to the boilers that his shabby overalls, his clogs, his waterproof jacket, and even his hair, became splattered with white.

Karol preferred to work the night shift. He said, that's when "there's less going on in the factory, and once the right quantity of lime has been delivered, I can spend time reading." And he did just that.

Some workers used to tease him when at midnight Karol knelt on the factory floor to pray. Once he asked the chief stoker for time off to attend a daytime mass. The man not only agreed, he finished Karol's work.

All this time Karol was writing poetry. Years later he published his poems under the pen name of Andrzej Jawien, in the independent Catholic weekly *Tygodnik Powszechny. The Quarry* shows that Karol felt every person is unique and all work is important. He wrote:

> . . . *Hands are a landscape. When they split,*
> *the pain of their sores*
> *surges free as a stream.*

But no thought of pain—
no grandeur in pain alone.
For his grandeur he does not know
how to name . . .

Karol faced danger every day. As if the job at the Solvay plant, his secret classes and theatre rehearsals weren't enough, he became active in a movement to help Jews. Few people knew that Karol travelled to neighboring towns to find safe hiding places. He helped falsify identification papers and to disguise Jews so they could escape to other countries. When the war ended Karol helped to organize care for Krakow's Jewish cemetery.

In the winter of '41 Karol's father suffered a heart attack. He had to remain in bed. So Kydrynski's mother cooked meals which Karol reheated at night. One day Karol came home to find his father dead. Twenty years old, he was an orphan. His closest companion was gone. Grief-stricken, Karol prayed next to his father's body for the next twelve hours. Abruptly at this point, Karol changed his life.

He spent more time alone. He prayed and studied more. He visited his father's grave every week and stopped going to rehearsals. One day he told Kotlarczyk not to cast him in any more roles. He decided that the Lord had a program for him. He would become a priest.

24

❧ 4 ❧

Training and the Priesthood

Taking training to become a priest proved to be very difficult. The Nazis had banned all education. That included religious instruction. The Gestapo had imprisoned and killed thousands of clergy. Moreover, they threatened to kill or send any religious students they discovered to Auschwitz. Still Karol persisted.

At first he tried to join the Carmelite order. But they told him, "You are meant for greater things." Determined, Karol decided to study with the underground while continuing his work at the Solvay factory.

At this time, after three years under German rule, Poland had become a starving nation of seemingly quiet people. Then came a surprise.

During World War II the Soviet Union had broken with Germany and become an ally of the United States

Young Father Wojtyla was popular with his students. He believed that lessons could be learned under the trees—or in kayaks.

27

and Britain. Now the Russian army advanced into Poland until it was within 40 miles of Warsaw.

Moscow radio told the Poles liberation was near. They felt stronger. Believing the Russians to be on their side, they took up arms. Food, weapons, and ammunition were scarce, but they fought hard. It took the Nazis 63 days to put down the Polish revolt. The Russians never came. When the shooting ceased Poland had lost 200,000 brave people.

The Germans sought revenge. They leveled Warsaw, and in Krakow on Sunday, August 6, 1944, Nazis went crazy. Gestapo and SS units swarmed over the city. They dragged people outside and shot them in the street. They searched house by house for all men between the ages of fifteen and fifty. Shots rang out all day. Alone in his apartment Karol prayed. Somehow on the day now remembered as *Black Sunday,* Karol was spared. Although his door was unlocked the Nazis did not search his house.

Cardinal Sapieha was courageous. He could have fled the country. Instead he stayed to help his people. Now, he decided, it was time to protect several young priests-in-training. As a priest he was supposed to remain neutral, but as a Pole he wouldn't.

He summoned Karol and nineteen other students to the palace. They removed their clothes and put on the black cassocks of priests. They turned the spacious living room into a dormitory, and there they ate, studied, and slept for the next two years. No one dared leave.

If you were caught without proper papers, it meant death. No one knew whether a knock at the door would bring enemy or friend. Everyone lived cautiously.

One day Cardinal Sapieha had the local governor to tea. The German viewed several rooms, unaware that "wanted" students lived only doors away.

The cardinal served the German governor on family heirloom plates of fine porcelain with gold filigree designs. But he offered only the same bread and jam all Poles were forced to eat every day.

Moving into the palace put Karol in a dangerous position. Because he had stopped going to work, the company listed his name with the Germans. When warning letters began to pile up at his old address, Cardinal Sapieha arranged with the factory manager for Karol's name to accidentally be 'lost'. Thus Karol mysteriously disappeared from Nazi scrutiny into his spiritual studies.

When the war ended Poland counted over six million citizens dead. The country looked like a "smashed graveyard." Homeless people searched for family members. Food, clothing, tools, all necessities, were scarce. Cities had to be rebuilt. Yet somehow Krakow had escaped with little destruction. But nearby, Auschwitz told the full story.

In Auschwitz, gallows and graves, human ashes and bones, piles of clothing, were everywhere. Years later when Karol was first bishop, then cardinal, he celebrated mass several times at Auschwitz in memory of the four million people who died there.

In 1945 Jageillonian University reopened. Karol entered and wrote a paper on St. John of the Cross, which he completed with honor. Impressed with his ability, his professor gave him a grade of excellent-plus.

Finally on November 1, 1946, Cardinal Sapieha ordained a happy Karol in a private ceremony. Pleased to begin his life work, Karol (now Father Wojtyla) celebrated his first mass in the Wawel cathedral chapel he loved so much. Within days he celebrated three private masses for his parents and his brother. Then he returned to Wadowice where, after saying mass, he shared lunch with old friends. All of Wadowice was proud of him.

Because Cardinal Sapieha realized Father Wojtyla was an unusual man, he wanted him to go into the world, to experience new things. So he paid the expenses to Rome, where Wojtyla studied at the Angelicum University for two more years. Here Wojtyla tackled the most difficult questions. He enjoyed making them easily understood. When he took exams for his doctoral degree he received a perfect score.

On weekends he worked with emigrants, helping them resettle into a new country. On holidays, with fellow priests, he traveled to Belgium, France, and Holland. Remembering what it had been like working in the quarry, he talked easily with young working people.

On one trip, he wrote to a friend: "Each day is filled to the brim with activities. This gives me the feeling that I am serving God to the best of my abilities and according to His will."

Wojtyla returned to Poland during its darkest hours. Under Wladyslaw Gromulka, Poland was trying to remain independent. But Stalin's Communist repression replaced Nazi tyranny. Once more innocent people were being arrested and persecuted unjustly. Again people feared the police, and the prisons were filled.

The church signed an agreement with the state that permitted religious education in schools. On paper it looked good. Actually there was little freedom permitted the church.

Father Wojtyla was made vicar of the rural village of Niegowic. Located on a river flat, its red brick church was in bad condition. Its rickety wooden bell tower was ready to fall down. During his year's stay in Niegowic Wojtyla encouraged the villagers to build a new church.

One old man recently said, "He was always wanting to do things for you. Nothing was too much trouble at any time of the day or night."

Wojtyla altered the village Christmas tradition. It was customary for the children to sing carols in people's homes. The serenaded families in turn contributed money to the church. But Wojtyla gave the collected offerings to the poor. Once someone gave him a beautiful feather quilt. After accepting the gift politely, he presented it to three girls who had just lost their mother. He cared little for material things.

In 1949 Father Wojtyla was transferred to the St. Florian parish in Krakow. His aunt Stefania who had no children of her own, came to keep house for him. She adored her nephew but the constant activity in the house annoyed her. Once she lost patience when Wojtyla returned from one movie, only to immediately rush off to another with beloved students following.

During these years he taught religion, preached, visited parishioners and still found time to dress in ordinary clothes and play soccer with the children. He performed over 200 baptisms and 160 marriages within two years. University students flocked to his house for lively talk.

People either thought his sermons were too long or they were greatly impressed by them. Certainly his acting and elocution classes helped. His deep voice held people's attention. And in spite of the Communist regime making religious study unlawful, Wojtyla encouraged youngsters to assist in services.

After three years he took a partial sabbatical. He returned to the Jageillonian University and continued to work at St. Florian. His second doctoral dissertation was about Max Scheler, a man who believed it is not what a person is, but what he does and becomes, that is important. In 1953, when the university made him a junior professor, his students lovingly called him "the eternal teenager."

Soon after, a dean from the University of Lubin, the only Roman Catholic university in Eastern Europe, invited Wojtyla to lecture there. His zeal, his original thinking, impressed the faculty. They invited him to lecture on a regular basis.

Busy as a parish priest, a teacher, an organizer of various student activities, Wojtyla managed it all by commuting via train overnight between the two cities— Lubin and Krakow. When he was 36 years old he became a full professor at the Institute of Ethics at Lubin. He held this position even when he became a bishop in 1958.

Wojtyla was a popular teacher. Students filled his classroom to overflowing. He talked; he encouraged. He preached ideas which did not agree with positions held by Poland's Communist government. He asked questions and listened to students' answers. He respected all opinions.

A friendly man, at dinner he loved to roll back his chair onto its two back legs and open discussions on every subject. Students talked about sports, ethics, philosophy, and especially the theatre.

One Spring day a trip came about because one student said, "The crocuses are in bloom at Zakopane."

No one, including Wojtyla, had seen the mountains covered with crocuses. So they arranged to go. At the appointed hour only the girls appeared. The boys could not make it.

Father Wojtyla, dressed in his hiking knickerbockers, looked like a civilian. But people did not think it proper for a priest to take girls on an overnight trip alone. To avoid trouble, the girls solved the problem by calling him "uncle" and the nickname has stuck ever since.

Thus it became a yearly experience. Uncle organized student journeys. They hiked together. They bicycled, skied, canoed, and paddled kayaks. They visited several cities. Usually trips lasted for two weeks.

They travelled about 200 miles. Girls carried packs weighing 30 pounds. Boys carried more. Uncle especially liked to hike to the lakes in the Koszalin province.

When they camped, he woke before anyone else. He liked to canoe alone when the air was fresh, the birds were just waking, and the water was still. Every morning he said mass. He used a turned-over boat for an altar and formed a cross by lashing two paddles together.

Often after swimming Wojtyla would sit on a log and hold class with pupils stretched out on the grass nearby. Even when he became bishop of Krakow he continued to teach. But then students travelled as far as 110 miles to crowd into his tiny Krakow flat.

Today as pope and head of the Roman Catholic Church he is still a professor of the Lubin University.

He likes to say that now his students have to come to the Vatican for seminars. For all of his teaching years, Wojtyla refused to accept a salary. Instead he has insisted that the money he would have earned be used to establish scholarships for poor pupils.

On the camping trips Father Wojtyla led, everyone would gather by the campfire in the evening to sing songs. They sometimes made up songs about each other. Then, after prayers and hymns, they settled into sleep.

On the earliest camping trips, because no one could afford good camping equipment, they slept on bicycle tires instead of air mattresses. Some campers used big cloth sacks to sleep in since they didn't own proper sleeping bags.

❦ 5 ❧

The Teacher and the Cardinal

U ncle organized his students into captains and crews for their boating trips. The more experienced ones sat astern and steered. The girls usually crewed. The group ended the trips with a tea party in Krakow—where they started planning their next adventure.

In July, 1958, Wojtyla was kayaking when he was called back to Warsaw. Cardinal Wysznski wanted to make him the assistant bishop of Krakow. After accepting, Wojtyla asked, "This doesn't mean I can't continue my kayak trip, does it?"

It did not, so he rushed back to his friends and continued down the rapids. Twenty years later, on his last group trip, he proved he is still physically fit. Wojtyla

Even when he was a bishop, Karol Wojtyla did not give up camping trips with his students. He believed young people were the hope of the world—a belief he still holds.

swam 99 yards across the lake and back without stopping.

Wojtyla became bishop in trying times. Two years earlier, on a June day, factory workers had marched through the streets of Pozan. Carrying banners and posters they chanted, "We want bread. We want lower prices." The march began peacefully but feelings soon changed. More posters appeared. These read, "Down with the Russians. We want freedom!"

Suddenly people attacked the police. Shots were fired. Some women and children were killed. Three tanks, and buses of soldiers arrived. The crowd cheered and shouted, "Poles don't kill Poles."

A stray bullet killed an infantry officer. People draped Polish flags over the sides of Army buses. Workers took over the tanks. The fighting spread.

Crowds came to the city center, singing patriotic and religious songs. Some people looted shops and burned cars. Others turned trams into barricades. More troops and tanks arrived. By evening the uprising was over. But the world knew how bitterly the Poles were fighting for freedom.

The Communists imprisoned over 2,000 bishops, priests, and lay people. They confined Cardinal Wysznski to a monastery. They were determined to subdue the Poles.

When Stalin died, Poland's government softened the state-church restrictions. Again they permitted religion to be taught in schools. There was talk of a "Polish Spring," a reawakening of hope for better times ahead.

Gomulka, Poland's Communist leader, was in a tight corner. He knew Poland was surrounded by Soviet-dominated nations. He wanted his country to be independent. But to keep peace, to survive, he also knew it had to be friendly with the Soviet Union.

Tensions ran high. In villages, peasants divided the land among themselves. In cities, people were restless. When Cardinal Wysznski gave his first sermon in three years, he said the twentieth century had seen terrible persecution. But he felt people would endure if they could feel freedom, justice, and respect. He reminded the Poles to "speak less of rights and more of duties."

Wojtyla was ordained bishop on September 28, 1958, during this disturbing period. Again the ceremony took place in the Wawel Castle cathedral. He was 38, and the youngest bishop in Poland's history.

As the archbishop placed the mitre on his head, it is said that unexpected bright rays of sunshine shone through the stained glass windows. A friend he had worked with at Solvay during World War II interrupted the service. He said, "Lokek, don't let anyone get you down!" Everyone including Wojtyla, smiled.

Wojtyla wanted to remain in his small apartment. Church officials felt he should live in the palace. So one day while he was out of Krakow, they moved his books and few other belongings to the palace. Wojtyla was displeased and let them know it. He refused the huge bedroom with its valuable furniture, choosing instead a much smaller room.

Wojtyla worked hard and expected others to work

hard, too. He asked for precise facts. He demanded people use their time wisely.

Wojtyla never learned to drive. He felt that was a waste of time. Instead, he turned the back seat of his car into a miniature office, complete with writing table and reading lamp.

One day the car's electrical system didn't work well. His driver suggested switching off the light so the car wouldn't stall. Wojtyla insisted they drive with the light on as long as they could. Eventually they reached Krakow as planned with Wojtyla working all the way.

Wojtyla rose quickly to high positions within the church. Within four years he became vicar capitular. Then, a year later, Pope Paul VI appointed him archbishop of Krakow. And in 1967 he became the second youngest cardinal in Vatican history.

Wojtyla cared nothing about clothes or money. Nearly penniless, he traveled to Rome to receive his cardinal's hat. The new robes he wore were a gift from the sisters of the Feliganki Convent in Krakow. He borrowed money for his other expenses.

On the way to the Sistine Chapel ceremony he suddenly realized that his socks did not match his red robe. He and his secretary tried to buy red socks in several shops.

"Let's go to the Santa Marta Convent," he said. "Maybe the sisters who do the cardinal's laundry there, will lend me a pair."

But they were too late. The sisters already had returned the red socks to the cardinal. So, standing in black socks, Wojtyla received his red hat. Later he said, "It wasn't too bad. I watched carefully and I saw two other cardinals wore black socks too!"

No matter whether he was bishop, archbishop, or cardinal, Wojtyla lived simply. His quarters in the old Krakow palace consisted of a large study and a tiny bedroom. A madonna and a Polish winter scene hung on a bedroom wall. Only a gayly patterned pillow brightened his worn bedspread. A rosary and a thermos were within reach of the bed. His worn black shoes were tucked under the bed. Everything was kept in its proper place.

Wojtyla was (and is) an early riser. He liked to wake at six and celebrate mass. Then, in the kitchen, he would either make a meal of scrambled eggs and some white cheese or of homemade egg noodles and milk. Perhaps because he has rarely had much food, he would eat almost anything. He fasted—and still does—on all prescribed days because, as he once said, "If the bishop doesn't set an example by fasting, who will?"

Rarely did Wojtyla listen to the radio or watch television. He preferred to read, to write, or to be with people. His habit of reading while carrying on a conversation disturbed some people. But he was always able to recall all that was said.

With all his duties, Wojtyla kept writing throughout the 1950s and 1960s. He published articles, poems, even a play, in the Krakow Roman Catholic paper

Tygodnik Powszechny. In his books, Wojtyla spoke about love, responsibility, marriage, and the family.

Wojtyla believed then—and still does believe—that people are free to choose how they will act. These actions will bring good or bad feelings inside. He believed further, that prayer helps, and that when people are silent and listen closely, they unite with God. The Communists did not agree with his ideas. They wished he would silence his pen—but they left him alone.

Ever busy, Cardinal Wojtyla visited almost every parish, no matter how small. Like any ordinary priest, he heard confession, performed wedding and funeral services, and baptized the children of friends. Remembering those who helped him during his life, he helped people in every way he could.

He liked to drop in on friends to chat. At Christmas he visited workers, including those at the Solvay plant. Usually he celebrated Christmas with Krakow actors. They received Communion and sang carols together.

Generally Wojtyla worked 15–18 hours a day. But he also gave himself time off to climb mountains or walk in the fresh air. In the winter, as a cardinal, he skied in Italy or Poland, often schussing down the steepest slopes of the Tatra mountains. One friend called him "the dare-devil skier of the Tatras."

Once someone asked, "Is it becoming for a cardinal to ski?"

Wojtyla replied, "It is unbecoming for a cardinal to ski badly."

One day while skiing near the Czechoslovakian border, a militia patrol stopped him. Wojtyla handed a patrol officer his identification papers. But dressed in shabby ski clothes, the officer failed to recognize him.

"Do you realize whose papers you have stolen?" the patrol officer growled.

Wojtyla tried to explain. He insisted he was himself. But the policeman continued, "A skiing cardinal? Do you think I'm crazy enough to believe that?"

Minutes later the matter was settled and an embarrassed patrol man apologized.

Another time when Wojtyla stayed at a rest home for priests in Zakopane, an elderly priest mistook him for just a sports-loving priest. He sent him on small errands which Wojtyla filled without a word. Months passed before the elderly priest learned who had done his bidding.

A man of the outdoors, when Wojtyla moved into the Krakow palace he did the natural thing. He brought his skis and canoe paddles along and used them until he became pope.

⊰6⊱

Nowa Huta-Vatican II

In 1966, one year before Wojtyla became a cardinal, Poland celebrated a thousand years of Christianity. The government tried to ignore this celebration.

It scheduled soccer games at the same time special masses were held. It planned bus trips for children to keep them from the ceremonies. Newspapers and television did not mention the religious events. It was a test of wills—the church versus the state. The majority of the people by-passed the state and attended church activities.

Archbishop Wojtyla opposed many state issues. He knew the people must show strength and unity. Nowa Huta, a nearby Russian-built town, helped the Polish cause.

The government built Nowa Huta as a steel manufacturing center. It provided bleak, concrete houses for its 200,000 residents, but decided this modern city did not need a church. The people disagreed.

This is the controversial modern church at Nowa Huta, near Krakow, on the day it was dedicated by Cardinal Wojtyla.

Every Sunday, thousands gathered in a small chapel or prayed in the open. Finally in 1957 the Russians promised a church, and a cross was put up as a pledge.

Nothing happened until the government decided to use the proposed building for a school. The people protested. They battled in the streets. Luckily no one was killed. Eventually determined citizens and Archbishop Wojtyla obtained a building permit. But no money or material was supplied.

On a drizzly day ten years later, a huge crowd knelt in mud for an open air service. The cornerstone which came from St. Peter's tomb in Rome, was laid. Then and for years afterwards, Archbishop Wojtyla said a Requiem Mass for the 400 Poles murdered by Nazis on nearby hills.

Over the next ten years people worked hard. Relying on their own hands, voluntarily they brought two million stones from mountain streams and their own homes to build the outer walls of the church. Nowa Huta became a symbol of Polish faith.

Finally on May 15, 1977, when Wojtyla was already a cardinal, he spoke at the dedication of the church before a crowd of 50,000 people. He said the church was not just a building but made up of living stones; that it was built "for the children and grandchildren and for guests coming from afar."

Within the church are statues created by Polish artists to remember those who died in concentration camps. One large figure commemorates Maximillian

46

Kolbe, a Franciscan priest who exchanged his life for a father of a family and died in Auschwitz.

Today thousands attend the 12 Sunday masses said at the church. The building is also a center where the crippled and dying can come for help, or to die in peace.

Wojtyla was an unusual cardinal. He did not mind shaking hands. He did not need the traditional bowing of council members to each other. His door was open to all. He saw people without appointments on a first come, first served basis. Sometimes a priest waited while an old woman talked about her troubles.

When the government forbade large gatherings, Wojtyla "stretched" the rules by organizing nearly 500 groups of only 15 to 20 people. Under his supervision they met, prayed together, and developed books for Roman Catholic education.

He held monthly seminars in the palace for actors, workers, students, priests, and nuns. Some church officials disapproved. Ignoring those who felt he was inefficient, Cardinal Wojtyla established his own style.

When the Communist government opened Poland's borders for travel, Wojtyla visited Rome several times. He came to all of the Second Vatican Council meetings and four of the Vatican *Synods*. At these meetings he and other bishops and cardinals exchanged information, searching for ways to operate churches well. He mingled with clergy from around the world. Many became his good friends.

At the Vatican, Wojtyla spoke out for priests to give themselves completely to service for others. He said the church must be a place for the "people of God." But he asked the church not to condemn the non-believers. He argued for freedom for all people and all nations, because without freedom there can be no justice.

The bishops and cardinals he met in Rome noticed his energy and clear-headed thinking. They laughed at his humor and admired the patient way he examined problems.

Over a four year period he served on many committees. One committee wrote "The Church in the World Today." The rules they set are similar to a constitution to direct Catholic life. Wojtyla helped plan sessions and guide debates. Through this work he became close to Pope Paul VI.

In 1970 he led 200 priests and five bishops, all ex-prisoners of concentration camps, to Rome. They came to celebrate Pope Paul VI's 50 years in the priesthood and to remember those who died during World War II. Six years later Paul VI asked Wojtyla to give Lenten retreat sermons before the cardinals. Some people feel the pope wanted them to measure Wojtyla's skills.

❧ 7 ❧

Pope Paul VI

Through the next decade Wojtyla extended his travel. He attended meetings in Australia and visited New Zealand, the Philippines, and New Guinea. He accompanied Cardinal Wysznski to Germany where the older cardinal asked for "cooperation and understanding;" for countries to look to the future and not the past.

He flew to Canada and the United States. Crowds loved his friendliness, his quick smile. He celebrated masses, gave lectures, and renewed friendships in many cities. He toured the Polish neighborhoods of Chicago, New York, Philadelphia, and Los Angeles. He rode through Hollywood, and with plate in hand, waited in line for barbecued chicken in Wisconsin. He patted cattle, saw horses, and blessed women, children, and landowners. He stopped to see a friend with whom he had corresponded. The friend lived in Great Falls, Montana.

Cardinal Wojtyla lived as simply as he could in his official residence. His study was not for show—it was a real workroom.

Like him, Jospeh Gluzek was a priest who had trained in Krakow and Wadowice. Gluzek showed his friend Wojtyla Montana's vast plains and beautiful mountains. And because Father Gluzek's congregation had never met a cardinal, Wojtyla said mass and blessed the babies.

At one point when given a list of three more meetings, he said, "No. I have to get some exercise." He cancelled the talks and went canoeing on the lake.

After speaking to seminary students at Harvard, *The Crimson* (the college paper) scooped the world. They said he could be the next pope. And 1978 proved to be his fateful year.

At the airport on his way home, Wojtyla suddenly jumped up. With cassock flying, he kicked his heels in the air like a happy schoolboy and shouted, "I'm going home!"

In August, 1978, Pope Paul VI died peacefully. His death had been expected. He had eaten supper as usual, recited the rosary, and had gone to bed. The next day he had a fever. He missed his usual appearance on the balcony. Another priest said the six o'clock Mass. The pope had lived and served. There was nothing left for him to do. Given Communion, he prayed until he died.

His body lay in state for two days, as thousands passed the open coffin. He was buried in St. Peter's under a statue of the Virgin Mary sculpted by Donatello.

He wanted to die "like a poor man." In his will he thanked God for the gifts and friends he had received and said, ". . . Everything comes to an end, and I must leave this wonderful and turbulent world. I thank you Lord."

So began the year of three popes.

Pope Paul VI had chosen the name Paul purposely. Paul or Pauline, means adventuresome, outgoing, and religious.

Pope Paul came to his post happily. But the workload was enormous. Sometimes he felt imprisoned. Nevertheless, during his reign he made important changes in the church.

Believing people pray more comfortably in their own languages, he finally ended the ancient tradition of the mass being said only in Latin. He wanted the church to serve all, especially the poor. He felt responsible for the Third World countries and said, "The Church could be the voice of those who have no voice." Once he sold a tiara (one of the papal crowns) and gave the money to the poor.

He started the Synods of Bishops in 1965 (yearly meetings, almost like a United Nations of clergy). Bishops came together to discuss church law, marriage, rituals, education, priesthood—the issues that could help the church bring greater justice to the world.

Paul VI spoke against the bombings in Vietnam and starvation in Biafra. World leaders, Mrs. Golda Meir of Israel, President Tito of Yugoslavia, Prime Minister

Edward Heath of England, and others, visited him. He, in turn, offered to meet with Communist leaders to try to improve life for Roman Catholics living under their rule.

Like Wojtyla, he believed priests must never marry, that they must devote their lives to the church. He left the question of women priests unanswered. Other beliefs were misunderstood. In the end, as he grew old, few listened. He left the unfinished work for his successor to carry on.

ᴈ8ᴈ

The Conclave

Electing a new pope is a serious and very secretive business. A previous pope never suggests a successor. It is a job the cardinals do alone.

The conclave, or series of secretive meetings, began the day Pope Paul VI died. No one knew how long it would last. It was the largest conclave ever assembled. Of the 111 cardinals, 56 came from Europe. There were 27 Italians, 12 from Africa, 13 from Asia and Oceania, 19 from Latin America, and 11 from North America.

Because they had met previously at Synods and other meetings, they were not strangers to each other. Dressed in their red robes, they met in the Sala Bologne on the third floor of St. Peter's.

Already the general, pre-conclave assembly had caused problems. Sixteen cardinals were over eighty. The eighty-two-year-old Archbishop Lefebre of France

The crowds in Rome know that a new pope has been elected when a puff of white smoke rises from the stovepipe of the Sistine Chapel. This message to the world comes from a rather small stove (see inset).

told a French reporter, "If I were elected pope it would be one of the greatest miracles of all times."

He objected strongly when some cardinals said that those over eighty should not be permitted to vote. He felt that would be like being put to death, if his wisdom could not at least be heard.

The press jumped on every rumor, every statement they could tell the rest of the world. They told of cardinals quarreling among themselves. They ran after cardinals for statements.

Andrew Greely, an American priest and writer, said, "The Catholic Church needs as its leader a holy man who can smile." He said he would not mind having a woman pope or *papessa*. "A papessa could not make more of a mess of the Church than we men have done over the last 1900 years. Viva la papessa!", he said.

Pope Paul VI had hoped the conclave would be a time of quiet and prayer. But cardinals are human. Discussions grew heated. Around and around it went. Different cardinals were mentioned for different reasons. One candidate after another was ruled out.

The Latin Americans had their man. The Europeans had theirs. The name of Cardinal Albinio Luciani of Venice, was rarely mentioned. Perhaps because they did not quarrel about him, he began to feel like the right choice.

The cardinals decided the new pope would have to be tough on human rights. He would want to keep the church traditions—the right to life for children (no abortion), priests remaining celibate or single, no women priests. Feelings for an Italian *pastorial bishop,* one who believed in the poor and local churches working in communities, grew.

Luciani seemed about the right age, under sixty-five. He was holy and learned. He lived without pomp. He wrote and spoke in a popular style. He opposed Communism. He was against divorce. Was he the right one?

Reporters could learn nothing. Every rumor they tracked down was denied. The Vatican press office closed at two. The reporters protested and things improved. The press office stayed open longer. More telephones were installed, and five reporters saw the conclave quarters. But important news remained a secret.

Each cardinal swore in advance that no matter whom they elected, each would defend the liberty of the Holy See, or pope. On August 25th the conclave opened with a mass. Then reporters saw cardinals leave the hall two by two. They burst into applause for Cardinal Wysnzski and for others they recognized. When the last two departed, they relaxed, knowing it would be a while before white smoke came from the papal chimney.

That afternoon the cardinals met in the Pauline Chapel before entering the grand Sistine Chapel. Dressed in red cassocks, white surplices, red mozzettas or shoulder capes, and red birettas, they were a splendid sight.

The special stove stood in the left corner of the room. Scaffolding protected the world-famous, painted frescoes by Michelangelo. The floor was covered with a beige wool rug. Cards on the two long, narrow tables marked each cardinal's place. Each chair was covered with red velvet. The straight chair backs and the hard seats made sitting uncomfortable.

After prayers, the TV crews were ordered out and the doors were sealed. Cut off from the outside, except for a telephone to use in an emergency, the cardinals were alone. They did not vote the first night. Instead they studied the papal constitution. They took their oath and vowed never to "break the secret in any way."

The cardinals slept in rooms called *cells*. Some were placed in little offices with faded wallpaper. Others were housed in rooms with ceilings forty feet above. The most frail, and the oldest, stayed in rooms close to the Sistine Chapel. All telephones were unplugged.

Furnishings were simple—a narrow bed, a red shaded lamp, a wash basin, kleenex, writing paper, and a small table. All shutters were closed. Windows were locked. There was no way to receive messages. There were only the cardinals and God.

One cardinal said, "It was like living in an airless tomb."

Only eleven cardinals had taken part in another conclave. On the second morning they held a short meeting. Then, disguising their handwriting, they wrote their choice on a ballot. They folded the ballot in half and then knelt at the altar. They told God this was the one they felt He would elect. Then they placed the paper in a silver *chalice,* the ceremonial cup used in celebrations of the mass.

After everyone voted, the papers were shuffled. Each was opened and counted by three "scrutineers." Then they were threaded together and burned, two at a time.

Albinio Luciana surprised everyone by gathering a few votes on the first ballot. By the second count, he had enough for a majority. When the final tally came in, he had well over the needed 75-plus-one vote. He was to be pope!

But who was he?

Everything happened so quickly. The famous stove was lit at 6:25 p.m. Vatican radio announced white smoke appeared at 7:15 p.m. People wondered. They received the news quietly. While the cardinals knew and respected him, he was unknown to the press and public.

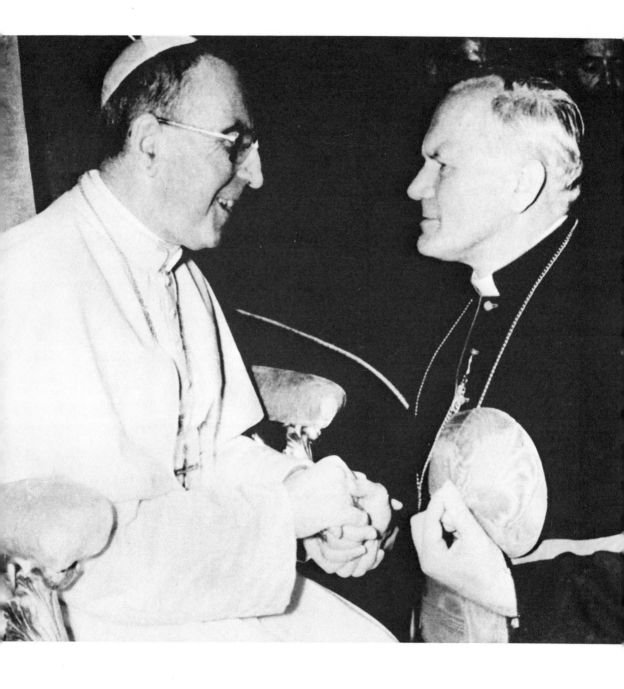

❧ 9 ❧

Pope John Paul I

Albino Luciana had grown up poor. His mother wrote letters for people who couldn't read, and worked as a maid. His father sometimes worked in a glass factory in Murano, Italy. When he couldn't find work in Italy, he took jobs in Germany or Switzerland as a brick-layer or electrician, and sent money home.

Luciana became a priest to help the poor. He studied for the priesthood in 1935 when Mussolini was in power. Like Wojtyla, he took his doctoral training in Rome. On returning home, he traveled to many surrounding villages. By doing various jobs, he became a *generalist*. Eventually he taught in a seminary.

Always ready to welcome priests and parishioners, he felt "a priest . . . is a man for all." He believed the church belongs in the community. He encouraged young priests to see different countries. A country boy at heart, he believed truth should be the center of one's life.

Pope John Paul I greets Cardinal Wojtyla in an audience. Neither man could know that Wojtyla would soon be called John Paul II.

He selected the name John Paul for two reasons. Pope John had made him bishop and Pope Paul VI had made him a cardinal. But he refused to have the tiara (the papal crown) placed on his head. Pointing out that the pope was one of the people, he kept the ceremony simple.

Instead of receiving the crown, he accepted a *pallium.* Made from lamb's wool, this Christian symbol usually is placed on a bishop's shoulders. It suggests that to serve others is not an easy job.

Pope John Paul was the first pope to come from a working class family. He brought a simple life to the Vatican. He lived quietly. He ate little except when he dined with guests. He worked hard all day and was in bed by nine. He loved children, fishermen, workers, all people. He told everyone to "think of me as God's postman."

Pope John Paul liked to walk the streets incognito. Dressed as a priest, he enjoyed going into local restaurants and talking with the crowds.

At conferences he loved to practice speaking English. He was neither humble nor conceited. He just lived.

Pope John Paul proposed several ideas that opened the way for changes in the church. He suggested that the richer churches give 1% of their income to the poor churches, and the Third World. He called this "the brother's share."

About the world's first test-tube baby he said, "If the

parents acted in good faith, with correct intentions, they may have great merit before the Lord." But he wondered if science would misuse this process as time passed.

He worried about science and the use of technology. He felt the world had forgotten brotherly love. And he said that without caring for each other, the world could be reduced to a desert. He was thinking about ecology, nuclear wars, and dictatorships. He wanted all Christians to unite for peace.

Like Pope Paul VI and Wojtyla, he believed priests must remain single. He praised the family and pushed for human rights. But his speeches were unexpected.

Was he in favor of parents deciding whether or not to have children? Did he believe qualified women should be allowed to preach? People interpreted his words the way they felt they had heard them.

Pope John Paul knew he did not understand the problems of other nations well. But he felt a world or-organization could work for peace and justice.

Throughout his life he had been sickly. He had been in the hospital eight times, and operated on four of those times. Each day he found his duties growing heavier.

One month after taking office, on September 29, 1978, at 5:30 a.m., his secretary knocked on the bedroom door. He wondered why the pope had not come to mass. Inside, the lights were still on. But the pope was dead. At about eleven the night before, he had suffered a massive heart attack. Just before retiring, he had said, "Even young people are killing each other now." Those are his last recorded words.

After a brief month of his presence, rejoicing ceased. People mourned again. It rained the day of the funeral. People wept openly, passing by the coffin. One reporter wrote, "Even the heavens wept." The 95 cardinals attending services had not expected to return to Rome so soon.

Feelings at this second conclave were different. Saddened by the pope's death, now the cardinals wanted a man with stronger energy. They still sought an Italian, but did not rule out someone from outside Italy. They felt they had to chose someone healthy.

Should he be in his 50's? Should the length of service be limited? They decided that like John Paul, the new pope must be *pastoral* or for all people. Some cardinals felt John Paul I had opened a new era. He had done God's will and left.

Outside the Vatican, streets looked like a Sunday carnival. Crowds bought candy, ice cream, and helium-filled balloons. Once in a while, when a child's balloon sailed skyward, people cheered.

"Determined smoke-watchers" set up camp stoves and cooked while waiting. At night a city searchlight beamed on St. Peter's Square. Television and radio people set equipment atop the famous colonnade.

By Monday the crowd thinned. It was a work day. Then smoke curled from the Sistine Chapel flue. Once more the world had a new pope. Whom had the cardinals elected this time?

Wojtyla heard the news of John Paul I's death in Krakow. Stunned and upset, he stayed alone for three days in his private chapel.

He was worried. He remembered that at the conclave which elected John Paul I, the cardinals had cast seven votes for him. Remote as it seemed, he sensed that he might not return to his beloved Poland.

At the funeral of John Paul I, Wojtyla said the dead pope had "great simplicity, modesty, respect for all people." And he concluded, "If Christ wanted him to be Pastor . . . on earth for such a short time we can only accept the will of Providence."

Before leaving for Rome, a frail old woman asked Wojtyla's help. Some people had taken her beloved cat away. He drove the woman to the spot, retrieved her cat, and then drove to the airport.

When reporters followed him in Rome, he said, "Don't worry. They won't want me. It's going to be another Italian." But friends feel Wojtyla already suspected what might happen.

The second conclave was just as secretive as the first. Reliable sources said there were quarrels and problems. It seems the two most popular Italian cardinals could not collect the 75-plus-one votes needed. The cardinals deliberated two days. After eight ballots, on October 16th they elected Cardinal Wojtyla.

The cardinals knew everyone expected an Italian.

But when they could not agree, after much deliberation, they elected the man they felt was the most capable.

At fifty-eight Wojtyla was strong and fit. He had contributed much to four Vatican Council sessions. He had served well on important committees. He believed in church traditions that were nearly twenty centuries old. His world-wide travels gave him appreciation for all people. Having lived under a dictatorship, he knew what life without freedom means. He had helped the Vatican write a document defending freedom of religion as a basic human right. He told the council that the church must work with the world to solve problems and bring dignity to all. The cardinals knew his poems, his articles, books, and play. This man could take on the heavy workload. Filled with hope, he would inspire everyone.

After counting the last vote, the conclave burst into applause. Wojtyla wept. He accepted the inevitable as God's will. He said John Paul would be his name to remember the pope of 33 short days who had prayed for peace and justice in a violent world.

After prayers, John Paul II changed into a fresh papal robe. He blessed the kneeling cardinals and prepared to meet the public.

Outside a huge crowd gathered once more. Looking to the chimney they shouted, "Bianca, bianca," as smoke poured out at 6:18 p.m.

❦ 10 ❦

The New Pope

St. Peter's Square was ablaze with light. A tapestry was thrown over the balustrade of the balcony. Assistants emerged. Under the glare of television lights Cardinal Felici said, "We have a new pope." More than 200,000 people roared. Some cried, others sang. Then the cardinal announced his name, "Carolum Cardinalem Wojtyla," and the cheering ceased. Where there should have been applause there was silence.

Whoever he was, the crowd loved that he'd taken the name of John Paul. But they knew nothing about him. One reporter said, "My God, he's a Pole!"

Frantically they asked each other, "Who is this man?"

Others asked, "How old is he?"

"Is he a Communist?"

"Why *not* a Pole? The church is universal. He is not a Pole any longer. He is our pope."

Frozen silence gave way to gaiety. The new pope ap-

Pope John Paul loves people. At big public gatherings in Rome, and most other places he goes, it seems he wants to reach out to everyone.

71

peared on the balcony with cardinals on both sides. He seemed shy and waved stiffly. The cheers died down. Speaking in Italian, he said, "Dilettissimi fratelli e sorelle!" (Dearest brothers and sisters!)

Delighted shouts, applause, spread across the square. Those who had feared the new pope would not speak Italian enjoyed his strong voice and almost perfect accent.

John Paul II's speech was brief. He told of being afraid to accept the job but he did so in "obedience to the Lord." Then he added, "If I do not explain myself well in your—our, language, if I make a mistake, you will correct me."

The conclave had elected the first non-Italian pope in four and a half centuries and the Italians loved him! "If he's the pope, he's Italian," they said.

Everywhere the surprise election was greeted with pleasure. Telegrams, letters of congratulation poured into the Vatican from leaders of nations around the globe. Poles who had emigrated to other countries walked tall with pride.

In Poland, people flocked to the streets. Overjoyed, they laughed, cried, danced, and hugged each other. Church bells rang continuously. Somehow, Poland's long history of suffering and of steadfast loyalty to the church seemed to have been rewarded. A son of Poland had been chosen to lead the Roman Catholic Church.

Thousands came to his tiny apartment on Franciszkanski street. Thousands more held a spontaneous mass and sang hymns outside the cathedral of Wawel.

One Krakow student sadly said, "He was our friend. Now he has gone to be a friend of the world."

A Polish woman said, "He is gone from us but he will stay in our hearts."

At first the Polish government was quiet. Eventually they too wired congratulations. Then they lifted travel restrictions so that 5,000 people traveled by train, another 1,000 flew to witness the coronation.

October 22, 1978, was a mild autumn day. Over 300,000 persons, including many world leaders, jammed into St. Peter's Square. Millions more witnessed the ceremony on television.

Like the first John Paul, the new pope refused to wear the triple crown tiara. Instead he wore the *miter* or much lighter headdress of bishops and cardinals. Standing on an altar surrounded by red and white gladioli, the colors of Poland, he accepted the *pallium* or lamb's wool yoke.

Refusing to be carried in the papal portable chair, at the close of the ceremony he walked directly to the group of visiting Poles. Speaking in Polish, he gave them a special message. Then he moved among the audience speaking in French, Italian, English, German, Spanish, and Portuguese. He shook hands and touched disabled people in wheelchairs. Finally he said, "It's time for you to go to eat as it is for the Pope."

Later that same afternoon he left the Vatican. Riding in his open car, with cheering crowds lining the streets, he visited his Polish bishop-friend André Marie Deskur who lay unconscious in a Rome hospital. (The bishop has since recovered.) With this action he showed everyone that as pope he did not intend to be a "prisoner" in the Vatican.

There has never been a pope quite like John Paul II. From the moment he stepped onto the balcony, people have been drawn to his warmth, his wit, his natural good manners.

An independent thinker, his blue eyes respond quickly. In seconds they can change from quizzical to amused, from sympathetic to stern or surprised. Built like a football player, his stride is heavy. His shoulders are slightly stooped. His big, square hands are roughened from laborer's work.

Although he never wanted or planned to be pope, John Paul II takes his job seriously and is clearly the boss. He became involved with all papal affairs immediately. He visits all offices, reviews issues, and has appointed officials a few at a time. He told a Polish friend, "I don't work any harder here than I did in Krakow. Only here I am constantly switching languages."

Unexpectedly he has visited workers and the poorer areas of Rome, as well as hospitals and schools. On impulse he has baptized and kissed babies, shaken hands, and hugged adults. Since he is bishop of Rome, wanting to stay close to the people as he did in Krakow, he visits local parishes on Sundays.

When a 22 year old daughter of a street cleaner asked him to officiate at her wedding, he did. Later in private he gave the couple a bible and two rosaries.

His Wednesday audiences draw such huge crowds that they have been divided into sessions and moved outdoors. At first he walked through a wide aisle to a large platform. Now, since audiences have increased, he has begun to ride slowly around the square in an open car. He will pause to take a hand, touch a cheek, accept a kiss, or listen to a child.

In December, 1978, conducting with his right hand, John Paul II led 50,000 Rome school children in Christmas carols. This may have been the first papal sing-along in history.

For a time a pop tune, written by a Netherlander, was a top seller. Called the *Wojtyla Disco Dance*, the words say:

> *Everybody talks about,*
> *Everybody sings and shouts,*
> *Looking out for the light,*
> *After such a long black night,*
> *He is nice, he's the man,*
> *The new pope in the Vatican.*
> *Many people love Allah,*
> *Other ones like Buddha,*
> *Some believe in Mohammed,*
> *Other ones just go to bed.*
> *But from Poland comes a man,*
> *The pope in the Vatican.*

If you go to the discotheque,
Shout 'Wojtyla' and stay awake.
Swing around and polka dance,
Up and down, it's romance.
He's the groove, he's the man,
The new pope in the Vatican.

During the summer John Paul II lives at Castelgandolfo, 15 miles south of Rome. A swimming pool was built especially for him. When a shocked Vatican official complained about the cost, the pope said, "It is less expensive than holding another conclave."

He takes a working vacation at Castelgandolfo. Sometimes he walks through the gardens or visits nearby convents and monasteries. Even here he holds private audiences, invites groups to early morning mass, and entertains.

On an August evening in 1978 he held a candlelight songfest for youth groups from Poland and Italy. Recalling his teenage years in Wadowice, he said, "A song is a way for being together, of communicating across language barriers."

After nearly four months in office, John Paul II took his first major journey. He traveled to the famous shrine of Our Lady of Guadalupe in Mexico. Legend says that the Mother of God appeared as a woman to an Indian called Juan Diego in 1531. Speaking the Indian *Nuahatl* language, she asked that a church be built in Guadalupe so she could stay near and protect the people.

When the pope's plane landed he knelt and kissed Mexico's soil. This gesture was to become a custom in every country he visited thereafter.

It is estimated that 18.8 million people saw him during this seven-day trip. He drove through the larger cities—Puebla, Oaxaca, Guadalajara, and Mexico City, and stopped in tiny villages. Banners, posters, houses decked with flowers welcomed him everywhere. Confetti rained down upon the streets. People sat up in trees, leaned from windows, lined the rooftops. Wherever he went, they greeted him with shouts of "Viva el papa!"

Protected by security officers and police escorts, he held an evening outdoor mass for 250,000 people. He celebrated masses with priests and nuns; he visited poor neighborhoods and talked with factory workers. He visited children in hospitals and schools. His auto stopped frequently, slowing the schedule as he encouraged people to talk.

In each city and town he talked against injustice and materialism (the ownership of too many things). He warned people not to forget God and asked them to help rid the world of hunger, poverty, bad working conditions, and illiteracy. Speaking in Spanish, he said, "Injustice hurts me . . . hate and violence cause wounds to humanity."

In Oaxaca Indians gave him a wide red stole with large white crosses at each end. They called him "little white feather" and "pope of the feather headdress"

77

after he wore part of a costume of a Zapotec dancer. He called them "his brothers."

His airport farewell was as noisy and colorful as his arrival had been. When the last waving stopped, after blessing the crowd he flew off to the music of La Golondrina." Tired, and tanned by Mexico's sun, the pope concluded a 15,500-mile, unforgettable journey.

⌒11⌒

Return to Poland

Five months later John Paul returned to his home-land. What a welcome his people gave him! Waiting patiently for hours, all over the country people sang, waved, prayed, and wept when he arrived.

As he knelt to kiss his native land, a 50-member military band played Poland's national anthem. Thousands cheered his triumphant motorcade ride to Warsaw. People lined up five and six deep along the streets. John Paul passed windows and balconies draped with papal flags of yellow and white, and the red and white flags of Poland. Often the crowd sang to him, "For he's a jolly good fellow."

John Paul wanted every Slav and Pole to hear him. Mary did. But the Soviet television showed only a two-second clip of his arrival and their press wrote only a two-sentence news report.

Everywhere he spoke carefully. When he met with government officials he criticized their farm policies.

When he came back to Poland as pope, John Paul II knelt in prayer at Auschwitz, the grim place where so many fellow Poles had died.

He defended the family, human rights, and religious liberty. He said the church wants to make people "more confident, more courageous." The church wants to make people aware of how creative and useful they can be.

With Cardinal Wyszynski, he prayed at the Warsaw tomb of the unknown soldier. And when the first mass ended, more than 100,000 voices sang, "God Bless Poland."

On June 4, 1979, he led a half-million pilgrims in an elaborate service at Poland's most popular shrine—the shrine of Our Lady of Czestochowa at the monastery of *Jasna Gora* (hill of light). Located outside the town of Czestochowa, thousands of Poles come to pray at the shrine of their centuries-old "Black Madonna," so called because of the darkness of the ancient icon image.

The pope called the shrine's power a mystery, a "force that touches the depths of hearts." As he had addressed the Oaxacan Indians, he called the bishops who concelebrated the mass with him, "brothers." He told them they must "work for human rights and that includes religious liberty."

A million people greeted him as he entered Krakow. The crowd shouted and sang *Sto-lat,* a Polish song that wishes a person 100 years of life. He asked them, "Do you really want your pope to live to 100?" When they yelled back, "Yes," he said, "Then let me get some sleep."

The following day John Paul returned to his birthplace, Wadowice. In front of the church where he had been baptized, he praised his religious teacher Father Zacher, his classmates, and all those who had helped him during his growing-up years. He prayed for the many dead, his family, and the sister who, born three years before him, had lived for only one day. Several times he asked the townspeople to pray for him.

After a formal service, the people of Wadowice enjoyed a lively family party. Relaxed and happy, John Paul joked and led 100,000 youngsters in a songfest of popular tunes. He sang encores with the crowd. Finally he half sang into the microphone, "Your buses are ready. Your buses are ready." Reluctantly the crowd took their leave.

One day he stopped at Auschwitz with survivors and priests who had lived in concentration camps. After praying in the cell of Maximilian Kolbe he flew by helicopter to Birkenau. Nearly a million people prayed with him among the camp ruins of twisted barbed wire, stark brick chimneys, and the few remaining original buildings. John Paul told the world that these camps are reminders of how far hatred can go.

The pope read memorial inscriptions of the 20 nationalities of people buried there. Of the Jews he said, "The very people who received God's commandment 'thou shall not kill', experienced in a special measure what is meant by killing." He wanted to visit his beloved Nowa Huta church but the government forbade it.

Finally on June 10th, he bade farewell to 2 million

people packed onto a huge Krakow field. People lined the middle of the road leading to the airport with flowers. Again huge crowds lined up for a last look. Cheering and weeping they wondered, would they ever see him again?

Before take-off John Paul knelt once more to kiss the Polish soil. A small group sang *Goralu Czy Ci Me Zai*, a Polish mountaineer's cry that asks: "Mountain man why are you leaving home? Why are you leaving the mountains of Tatra? Aren't you sorry to go?"

❧ 12 ❧

Old World to New

In September 1979, Pope John Paul undertook his longest journey. His first stop was in troubled Ireland where Roman Catholics and Protestants have been in active combat of one sort or another for a decade.

Here as elsewhere, it looked as if the entire country was turning out to meet him. Many families did what the family of a man called Alfie Parke decided to do. Alfie and his wife decided to bring their four daughters—ranging in age from two to nine—to see the pope. "It's one thing we can do for our children," they said. They waited through a damp night, a drizzly morning, and a blustery afternoon. Thousands of people stayed up all night, walked miles from parked cars, and huddled together in Dublin, Drogheda, and Knock—just to catch a fleeting glimpse of him.

The mood of the country was part picnic, part formal worship. Waiting for the plane's arrival, people sang hymns and clapped in rhythm to the music.

The pope has landed! John Paul II leaves the jet that carried him from Ireland to Boston. The papal coat-of-arms decorates the plane.

87

When the red papal helicopter flashed out of the gloomy sky—an hour late—they roared out their cheers.

John Paul was the first pope in history to step on the Irish earth he called "Island of Saints." Driving in his truck-like vehicle (which reporters nicknamed the Popemobile) throngs greeted him in song. Pouring out love and joy they sang, "He Has the Whole World In His Hands."

Nearly 1.2 million people attended his first mass in Dublin. Clapping, cheering, they sang partly in Gaelic, partly in English and Latin. Here he spoke of children being God's gift, about being good parents, and keeping families together.

He asked the Irish to turn from violence to peace. He said, "Do not follow those who train in ways of inflicting death." He urged respect for work in service and for love and respect of life. He appealed to terrorists to lay their arms aside. But he knew he was powerless to do more than make speeches.

Before flying off to the United States he said in Gaelic, "God bless and keep you forever." And the crowd responded with thunderous applause.

The pope's jetliner touched down in the United States in the rain. It poured on his several ticker tape parades. Rain drenched millions who waited for him. But nothing dampened people's joy everywhere as John Paul whizzed through his seven-day lightning-fast tour of America.

To Roman Catholics and non-Roman Catholics alike,

he became a shining "superstar" of the church. This athlete–sportsman kept a schedule that would have tired a man years younger. His smile, his gestures, his wink, his thick Polish accent, drew laughter and cheers everywhere.

Children were his favorites. Spontaneously he kissed babies or scooped up a child into his arms. He patted their heads and shook their hands. He told children they are "the future of our world."

Everywhere he drew enormous crowds. More than 400,000 people stood in torrential rains on the Boston Common. One million gathered for mass in Philadelphia's Logan Circle. Another half-million came to Chicago's Grant Park. People serenaded him with "Getting to Know You" and "He Has the Whole World In His Hands," or with the Polish national anthem.

Again and again he preached against materialism and for the rich to share their wealth with the needy. Many of his ideas could have been said by other religious leaders, but on this trip he was the star.

America's first lady, Rosalynn Carter, graciously welcomed him to Boston. On the Common 300 thoroughly drenched priests wading through thick mud to distribute communion to 60,000 people. Twelve nuns had baked the hosts for communion on a twelve-hour-a-day schedule for a week.

He reminded Bostonians that citizens of their city had hung a Quaker in the 17th century, and that Boston was once the center for religious persecution.

Showing how well he'd prepared his speech he quoted the words of John Winthrop, the first governor of the Massachusetts Bay Colony. Winthrop had written, "We must love one another with a pure heart. We must bear one another's burden."

Then John Paul added, "These simple words explain so much of the meaning of life—our life as brothers and sisters in our Lord Jesus Christ."

Later, just before leaving Holy Cross Cathedral, he paused at the only wheelchair in the church. Taking the hand of paralyzed Jane De Martino, age 26, he gave her a small box. Jane had been disabled in an accident. On opening the box inscribed with *Totus Tuus* (Totally Yours), Jane found a white rosary with a gold cross. She said, "If you had given me the whole world it wouldn't mean so much."

The pope called "America beautiful even if it rains." And a Boston official said, "It's almost like it was during the great blizzard two years ago. No snow—but people are aware of each other, reaching out."

In New York, police security was tight at all times. Police helicopters circled overhead. Police boats patrolled the river. Plain clothesmen mingled with the crowd. Secret service men watched him closely. Over 11,000 police worked twelve-hour shifts, some with trained dogs, to insure his safety. The police had good reason for being so cautious. The Newark FBI office had received a warning that the pope would be shot. A letter directed them to an apartment where they found a submachine gun and several handguns. But harming the pope was the last thing most people had in mind.

It rained on his New York parade. But dressed in a plastic raincoat and a broad-brimmed red hat, John Paul was prepared. Cameras flashed, banners waved, confetti and streamers were thrown into the air. John Paul touched hands anywhere he could reach. He covered his ears with good humor as the crowd shrieked deafening cheers. At one point when they yelled, "Long live the Pope," he responded with "You're right,"—an odd remark for a pope to make.

At the United Nations dignitaries from 152 countries waited in line to shake hands. Costumed children greeted him, reminding the world that 1979 was the International Year of the Child.

Silent delegates listened respectfully to his address. Again John Paul urged human rights, dignity for all people, and world peace. He asked for the preservation of Jerusalem as a holy city of all faiths. And he wondered whether armaments could serve world peace. He asked, "Are the children to receive the arms race from us as a necessary inheritance?"

He condemned torture and prayed that "every concentration camp anywhere on earth may once and for all be done away with."

Then his motorcade moved quickly from one part of the city to another on a whirlwind tour. It passed run-down brownstone houses and shops with barred windows. In every neighborhood he saw people dressed in their Sunday best.

In Harlem he listened to a gospel choir. One 71-year-old man said, "I don't believe it. I call this a miracle on 151st Street." And a black woman on Frederick Douglass Boulevard yelled, "Hey there, Pope!" Persons greeted him as they would a friend.

For a few short hours, streets usually filled with litter and street gangs were scrubbed and safe. Workers had spent nearly two weeks washing the streets and plugging potholes. They even demolished abandoned apartment buildings ahead of schedule.

In the Hispanic area of the South Bronx, Father Neal Connelly told him, "We are not surprised that you came. It tells the whole world that we (poor people) count." Long time Italian residents thought his coming to their Bronx neighborhood was a minor miracle.

In Yankee stadium an impatient crowd of 80,000 clapped rhythmically when he entered. Circling the field in his white Popemobile (a rebuilt Ford Bronco truck), the pontiff extended his arms from side to side in blessing. People felt compelled to wave back as though he was greeting each one of them individually.

This mass with a 50-piece band and a choir of 14,000 voices from Connecticut, New York, and New Jersey, ended the day's formal events. He told the assembled crowd, "The poor of the United States and the world are your brothers and sisters . . . You must not leave them the crumbs. You must treat them like guests at your table."

The next morning when he said an early mass in St. Patrick's Cathedral, nearby streets were closed to traffic. After services, John Paul joined the outside umbrella-laden crowd in song. After the singing was over, in a rich bass voice he said, "Ver-ry nice!"

Then he sped off to meet 19,000 teenagers dressed in blue jeans and t-shirts. Packed into Madison Square Garden, they went wild when he hoisted a young girl onto his car.

They gave him a guitar (which he plays), taped music, jeans and a t-shirt with red letters that read, *Big Apple* (meaning New York) *Welcomes Pope John Paul II* and the best gift of all—the promise to do thousands of hours of service.

Delighted, and shaking with laughter, he hummed along as a 100-piece band from a Brooklyn Catholic school played themes from "Battlestar Galactica" and "Rocky". They went wild again when he cooed *Woo-hoo—woo* into the microphone, Polish slang for "Wow!"

Then he stopped at the Battery to speak facing the Statue of Liberty. He praised the vast differences among American people and asked them to create a new dawn for greater liberty. Later at Shea Stadium he spoke in four languages—English, Italian, Spanish, and Polish. He blessed nearby states, New Jersey and Connecticut, and after a long pause, *Brook-leen* (Brooklyn). His mispronounced words brought loud applause. The man with the Polish accent charmed the city of every accent.

John Paul's final words before flying to Philadelphia were: "A city needs a soul if it is to become a true home for human beings. You, the people, must give it this soul."

❧ 13 ❧

America's
Heartland

Arriving late in Philadelphia, the city of brotherly love, the pope was hurried through streets packed with celebrating people. Wherever he went, he joked and waved greetings.

On Logan Circle, within the huge crowds, were thousands from the mid-Atlantic states. Standing near the birthplace of America's 204-year-old Declaration of Independence, John Paul said, "A sense of religion is part of America's heritage."

The next day, October 4th, he told an audience of 14,000 nuns, priests, and seminary students that he was their Vatican authority. He declared, "Priesthood is forever," and priests may not marry. They must serve only the church. Then, referring to ancient church customs, he said that the priesthood is only for males.

At the end of his talk, amid the cheers, many nuns

Celebrating mass outdoors in Iowa, Pope John Paul lifts up the ceramic chalice that was made for his visit by a local craftsman.

sat stony-faced. And nuns elsewhere who were training to be ordained, were bitterly disappointed. Many Roman Catholics who were hoping John Paul would modernize the Church were concerned. Would his words cause church disunity?

His next stop surprised people. It happened because the pope received a neat hand-written letter that touched his heart. It came from Joseph Hayes, a 39-year-old farmer-mechanic in Truro, Iowa.

Joe Hayes works in a farm machinery factory to earn enough money to keep his 90-acre farm going. He does farm chores after work. His wife feeds and waters 12 cows, tends their garden, and operates the hay baler at harvest time. His teenage son Mark and his two daughters Theresa and Rhonda, help run the farm, too. His oldest son Paul is away at a state school for the handicapped. The family works hard and enjoys their life together. Before their evening meals they take hands and pray.

Because Hayes is involved in a program called "Strangers and Guests Toward Community Heartland," he felt the pope would enjoy seeing a century-old rural farm parish. But he really wasn't expecting a reply to his letter. So when the acceptance came, it threw Truro and nearby Des Moines residents into a frenzy of activity.

One pottery teacher worked 110 hours to make a special chalice and paten for the papal mass, as well as a pitcher and bowl for the *lavabo,* the ceremonial washing of hands by the celebrant of the mass. Local carpenters built the altar and papal chair from salvaged 100-year-old barn beams. Volunteers from Wisconsin held a two week quilting bee to stitch together a ten foot square banner colored burnt orange, sky blue, and leafy green.

Met by Iowa's governor and the mayor of Des Moines, John Paul's first stop (by helicopter) was St. Patrick's, a tiny church with only fifteen pews. After talking quietly with the parishioners his helicopter took him next to the Living History Farm. Run by a private company, this unusual farm serves as a working model of past, present, and future farming methods.

The day was crisp and clear. Buses had brought people from Kansas, the Dakotas, Colorado, Wyoming, Minnesota, Wisconsin, and Nebraska. Teenagers, including 75 students from Independence, Iowa, who hiked 130 miles, were there to see him.

The mass was held in an open 180-acre field. It was rich with pageantry and song; families carried symbolic gifts—earth, garden tools, vegetables—to the altar. John Paul praised farming and called attention to the starving masses elsewhere. He told the farmers you "can provide food for millions who have nothing to eat and help rid the world of famine."

He said, "The farmer prepares the soil, plants the seed, and cultivates the crop. But God makes it grow. He alone is the source of life." He called America's heartland, "some of the best earth in the world," and added, "We must conserve the land for future generations. Iowa's farmland is God's Gift."

⊸ 14 ⊱

Washington, D.C.

From Philadelphia to Des Moines to Chicago, all in one day! Landing in chilly Chicago's airport, in the city with the second largest Polish population, again John Paul passed by enthusiastic crowds and billboards flashing bright signs of welcome.

Still weary after a night's sleep, and wearing a wrinkled cassock, he visited small dioceses before speaking at a seminary. He praised the 300 bishops there; and spoke forcefully for marriage and against birth control and divorce. He rejected mercy killings, and criticized the waste of resources. Once more he spoke out against preparing for war, and closed his speech with a plea for church unity. He said *love* is the best way to spread the word of God.

Then he topped off the visit with one more mass in Grant Park. Here the gathered 500,000 taking him at his word, turned the park site into a "love-in"

Even at the White House, Pope John Paul was able to cement relations with the young—and President Carter seems to approve.

with everyone caring for each other and John Paul.

The next morning his TWA 747 plane, the *Shepherd I,* flew to its final destination—Washington, D.C.

Washington, D.C. was the grand finale to an extraordinary week. Never before had a pope visited the White House. Former presidents had met previous popes at the Vatican. When John Kennedy ran for the presidency he had been forced to defend his Roman Catholicism.

Now more than 5,000 guests met two world leaders—a president and a pope—on the sunny White House lawn. John Paul shook hands with Congressmen, Supreme Court justices, governors, and other dignitaries. President Jimmy Carter greeted the pope with four Polish words: *"Niech bedzie Bos pochwalony!"* or "May God be praised!"

The pope, saying he came as a "messenger of peace and brotherhood," asked for an end to world hunger. And President Carter urged other nations and individuals to help the pope because it is the humane thing to do.

But Washington, D.C. was a scene of contrasts—there were jubilant crowds and there were banner-carrying pickets who demanded *Equal Rites For Women.*

At the National Shrine of the Immaculate Conception Sister Theresa Kane, president of the Leadership Conference of Women Religious, standing on the same platform as the pope, asked him to understand and to permit women to become "fully participating members" in all church duties. She meant priesthood for women among other things.

The pope listened quietly but gave no clue to his thoughts. When he spoke he did not answer Sister Theresa directly. Instead he pointed out that the Virgin Mary has served a major role in history. Yet she did not sit at the Last Supper. He reminded everyone that she is the honored spiritual mother and urged nuns to continue their good work.

Sister Theresa later said she had not expected the pope to answer. But because of his openness, she had felt comfortable enough to ask for future discussions. However, the next day, one embarrassed order of nuns advertised in a Washington newspaper. They apologized for Sister Theresa's "public rudeness."

The cold weather, the cloudy skies, and chilling winds did not keep the crowds away from the pope's final mass in the United States. It was held on the Mall. Half-frozen families kept warm in blankets and sleeping bags. Some sought shelter in nearby museums. The entire area between the Capitol and the Washington Monument looked like a "giant outdoor picnic."

Here the pope reminded the world that human life is God's precious gift. Selfishness weakens the family, and every family member must share hopes and burdens. He said, "Never lose sight of the things of the spirit. God gives meaning to our lives."

He concluded by asking God to bless America so that the country truly is "One nation under God, indivisible, with liberty and justice for all!"

❧15❧

A Tragedy

It had been a glorious week. Wherever he traveled people treated John Paul like a royal celebrity. He asked millions of Americans to lead better lives and to care about each other. Did they listen? Young people of Charlestown and Roxbury, Massachusetts, know that the pope's visit made a difference.

On Saturday, September 28, 1979, at half-time of an ordinary football game, a shot rang out. Fifteen-year-old Darrell Williams, a black athlete, fell to the ground. He had just completed his first touchdown for Jamaica Plain high school. Now he lay still with a bullet in his neck.

When the police arrested a few white teenagers near the stadium, they claimed it was an accident. They had been shooting at pigeons. Almost nobody believed them. Everyone seethed with anger. Race relations that had been bad for a long time, worsened.

Few black people walked easily through the white

On his return trip to Boston the pope learned that a tragedy had struck involving young people like these waiting to see him pass.

community of Charlestown. Likewise, few whites walked comfortably through the nearby community of Roxbury. Although some people had tried, no one had succeeded in making the streets safe in either area.

Merchants, the clergy, and the townspeople had ignored the growing hatred. They hoped it would go away. Quiet reigned only during the pope's visit. But John Paul talked about Darrell Williams and the communities' anger. Privately he suggested that Roman Catholic priests go into the community and try to bring about peace.

One priest said on television, "I didn't know how to begin. But I knew a boy and his mother were suffering. And everyone understands what suffering feels like." And apparently the priests did well, because suddenly black and white high school students were praying for Darrell. Young people began to collect money to pay for his hospital bill.

Jamaica Plain high school coach Tom Richardson said, "My team decided to be an example of the good that could come from a bad experience."

Parents spoke up. One mother said, "We want peace. We're sick of violence."

Students said, "We're in school to learn." And at the next game there was no trouble. Charlestown was remembering the pope's advice for people to understand each other.

❧ 16 ❧

A Changing Church

There has never been a pontiff like John Paul II. He appeals to people of all faiths. Praised by politicians, heads of state, private citizens, members of the clergy, he inspires hope and courage.

This journey to Ireland and the United States was a milestone in history! His speeches made the front pages of newspapers. His face appeared in the middle of almost everyone's television set. But people wonder. Can he change world conditions?

Forty years ago Karol Wojtyla was an ordinary Polish citizen, a potential slave of the Nazis. Forty years later he is the pope and head of the Roman Catholic Church. The Nazis are gone from Poland. But Soviet power, another tyranny in many people's eyes, remains.

The pope begins his reign during a painful period. The world is struggling with many issues. John Paul sees that some people are surrounded by material

The pope is a thoughtful man. In public as well as in private he weighs the modern world's problems and his role in solving them.

things—too many material things. And yet there is the constant danger of war and the horror of poverty and starvation despite the wealth of some. Nations threaten each other with nuclear armaments. Humans are tampering with the earth's natural environment. Half the world eats too much and owns too many things—cars, radios, televisions, houses, household machines, factories, etc. The other half is dying from malnutrition, disease, and lack of material goods.

Families struggle to survive. Many are splitting apart. Unhappy adults and children are turning to drugs. Yet at the same time new religious groups are springing up, showing that in their hearts, people want to believe in a world of peace and safety. Conflict and disorder exists everywhere, even within the Roman Catholic Church.

The papacy is founded on traditions that are nearly 2000 years old. Only a century ago the pope lived in the Vatican as a virtual prisoner of his high position. He never traveled. He often knew little of world affairs. Local churches acted upon rules sent from Rome.

Under John XXIII and Paul VI, with the establishment of the Vatican Councils of 1962–65, religious freedom expanded. Clerical dress changed. Local languages replaced Latin in church services. Lay people and clergy together developed guidelines for religious community life.

Several theologians, those people who study and analyze religious doctrines and beliefs, wrote books. They tried to make beliefs of the past workable in a modern world. For some, this period became an opportunity to reform the Roman Catholic Church. Other voices, fearful for the future, asked for a return to orthodox ways.

Vigorous protests from both camps grew very loud. Thus, John Paul came to the Vatican when the church was at a crossroad. Should it continue to modernize? Should it stay where it was? Or should it turn back the clock and rely solely on its past?

To many John Paul, like most kings and queens of today, seems to be a powerless monarch. Others see him as a truly powerful ruler who controls and guides his huge Roman Catholic flock.

Disagreement within the church is not new. Since the 13th century, the Vatican agency called the Sacred Congregation for the Doctrine of the Faith, has cross-examined and disciplined many who disagreed with established policies. Even Giovanni Battista Montini (later elected Pope Paul VI) once came under investigation. In 1933 he had to defend a critical letter he wrote against the church practice of collecting alms during Easter mass. Issues came to a head in December, 1979.

For several years, on and off, the Sacred Congregation has questioned several highly-respected priest-writers. Among them are Hans Küng and Edward Schillebeeckx. Who are these men?

Edward Schillebeeckx is a deeply religious Roman Catholic priest-scholar. Born into a middle-class family in Antwerp, Holland, on April 24, 1914, he attended a Jesuit high school. During World War II he joined the Dominican order in France. A teacher, he has lived a quiet, scholarly life. His carefully researched books about early Christianity are read and appreciated all over the world. Schillebeeckx wants the Christian message to become a living faith for today's society.

Like the pope he has experienced war and foreign occupation of his country. He remembers well how it feels to live without freedom.

When called to Rome, he came in spite of heart trouble. He answered all questions and cooperated fully with the Vatican committee. Before he left he proclaimed his complete loyalty to the Roman Catholic Church.

Hans Küng was born in Lucerne, Switzerland, on March 19, 1928. He was educated for the priesthood in Paris, Berlin, London, Amsterdam, Madrid, and Rome. He was ordained in 1954 in Lucerne. In 1962 Pope John XXIII appointed him to the Second Vatican Council.

A serious teacher, Küng has lectured at universities in Europe, Asia, North America, and Australia. Like the pope, he enjoys music and outdoor sports, especially skiing. A writer, too, his books have always stirred up controversy. Translated into about 100 languages, he is widely read.

Küng was skiing when the Vatican announced that it

had withdrawn his right to teach Roman Catholic doctrine at the ancient University of Tubingen in West Germany.

The decision caused an immediate international uproar. Clergy and lay people world-wide, rushed to his defense. Many did not agree with Küng's ideas but they wanted him to be able "to speak as he wishes."

The Vatican agency called Hans Küng to Rome several times. Without permission to bring a defender with him, feeling that secret questioning violated his "human rights," Küng stayed away. Küng feels he is a loyal Roman Catholic who wants to explore ideas and teach as he thinks.

Good, honest men—Edward Schillebeeckx, Hans Küng, and John Paul II—each has devoted his entire life in service to God.

The pope believes his first duty is to see that Roman Catholic doctrine is taught as it is written. He has said, "Teachers do not teach on their own authority. They follow church instructions and present personal opinions modestly."

He accepts Hans Küng as a Roman Catholic. And Küng may give public lectures if he says his ideas are his own opinion. Thus the conflict is over rights.

Küng can think as he chooses and teach his ideas. But he no longer represents the Roman Catholic Church. John Paul defends the right of Catholics to hear church philosophy clearly. Can these differing views operate side by side?

The Vatican Council Constitution says, "The faithful

shall have lawful freedom of inquiry, thought, expression . . . in whatever study they specialize."

Many devout clergy believe that when fine men do sincere research, they deserve to be encouraged rather than blamed. They would like to see Rome broaden its committee, adding a jury of peers to its bishops. The committee or agency would review and decide upon what the theologians discover. Investigations might still be held in secret, but making an annual report public would eliminate suspicion and build world respect.

❧17❧

Sto-Lat!

People wonder: What does the pope plan? Who is he?

At the United Nations he appealed to all governments. He asked for human rights, improved health, education, and housing—a better life for all earth's people.

His own life has inspired those silent worshippers living in oppressed countries—Czechoslovakia, Hungary, Yugoslavia, Rumania, and Bulgaria. To go to mass where church activities are prohibited or at best limited, takes courage.

Naturally warm and friendly, his zest and wit attracts people of all faiths. Spontaneously he may step into a crowd or visit a local parish church and talk with the parishioners. An author and a poet, he composed all of the major speeches for his world trip—sometimes singing as he wrote.

Disciplined and hardworking, John Paul is a person

John Paul II has been called "The Singing Pope." One of the gifts that pleased him most on his American tour was this guitar, presented by a student. Young people remain the center of his life and thought.

of action. He is a man who knows what he wants. Believing that the church operates from the top down, he expects complete obedience within the organized church.

Again doing the unexpected, on Good Friday, April 4, 1980, John Paul surprised the world. First he washed and kissed the feet of a dozen poor men who live in a home founded by Mother Teresa of Calcutta. (Mother Teresa won the 1980 Nobel Peace Prize for her work with India's dying and homeless.)

Then, covering his white papal vestments with a black silk cloak, he walked into St. Peter's unannounced. Taking the fourth confessional booth, he heard the confessions of 30 pilgrims, mostly from his native land, before the crowd realized history was being made. It was the first time a pontiff had listened to the confessions of ordinary parishioners.

Later, wearing the "maroon mantle of mourning," and carrying a simple wooden cross, he led the procession that symbolizes Christ's walk in Jerusalem almost 2000 years ago. At Rome's ancient Colosseum he paid homage to the early Christians put to death there.

Then on Easter morn, warning against the dangers of a godless society, he sent greetings in 33 languages including Chinese, Japanese, Swahili, Arabic, and, for the first time, Hebrew.

John Paul has known suffering. For 35 years he lived isolated from the rest of the world in a country dominated by a dictatorship. His life was shaped first

118

by the Nazis. Then the church became a foe of the Communists. Keeping it alive was a major feat. Somehow the Polish church united to maintain its orthodoxy and survived.

Some people see the pope as a traditionalist, a man who has old-fashioned ideas about women and the family. They are not sure he understands today's plural society. It is a society with many more cultures and life-styles than where he grew up.

Others see him as open and responsive, a man who educates himself by everything he does. They recall his stern speech in Puebla, Mexico. They remember how he told a large audience of Latin American cardinals, bishops, and priests that meditation and prayer were their first tasks. He said, "You are not political leaders. You are spiritual guides" who must help people live the love of God.

Then he went out and met the citizens. He saw the make-shift shantytowns and visited the rich and middle-class neighborhoods. He talked with rich and poor and changed his advice.

In his next speech he said, "The Gospel demands it to do all in its power to end injustice and make systems . . . more human." He urged workers to organize to improve their lives. He challenged Catholics everywhere to create a "civilization of love."

No figure in recent times has received more media coverage than Pope John Paul II. Regardless of ethnic or religious background, he is a man for all people.

119

Earthy and magnetic, he is the first Polish pope in history and the youngest in 132 years.

As an ex-soccer goal-keeper, a skier, a swimmer, a canoe and kayak enthusiast, a mountain climber, he appeals to sports lovers. As an author, poet, actor, a ferocious reader and participant in the Polish underground, he attracts intelligent and caring individuals. People are drawn to his joy and compassion and to the unexpected events that happen when he appears.

John Paul is a *personalist.* He believes in the value and the dignity of humankind. He is a man who has become a legend in his own time.

The institution of the papacy began centuries ago, and change comes slowly. Accepting new ideas takes a long time. What the pope's plans are, what he wants to do, no one really knows. The final surprise lies ahead.

But already John Paul has told the world that the Roman Catholic Church will help reduce suffering. Every day he reminds people in some way how wonderful it is to love God. He encourages the building of a world in which future generations may live in peace and prosperity and universal fellowship.

Sto-lat! May Pope John Paul live one hundred years.